LOVE POEMS

—— by ——

CHRISTINA ROSSETTI

LOVE POEMS

—— by ——

CHRISTINA ROSSETTI

PAVILION

First published in 1994 by
PAVILION BOOKS LIMITED
26 Upper Ground, London SE1 9PD

Produced, edited and designed by Russell Ash & Bernard Higton
Picture research by Mary-Jane Gibson
Text selection and design © Russell Ash & Bernard Higton 1994

This book is typeset in Monotype Perpetua

A CIP catalogue record for this book is available from the
British Library

ISBN 1 85793 458 X

Printed and bound in Italy by Graphicon

2 4 6 8 10 9 7 5 3 1

This book may be ordered by post direct from the publisher.
Please contact the Marketing Department.
But try your bookshop first.

CHRISTINA ROSSETTI 1830–1894

Christina Rossetti was born in London on 5 December 1830, the youngest member of a family notable for its artistic and literary interests. She was the daughter of Frances Polidori and Gabriele Rossetti (an Italian poet who fled to England as a political refugee and became Professor of Italian at King's College, London) and the sister of the writer William Michael Rossetti and the Pre-Raphaelite painter and poet Dante Gabriel Rossetti. Her talent for imaginative writing manifested itself precociously and she began composing verses as a child. Her first collection was privately printed when she was sixteen, and at the age of twenty she contributed – using the pseudonym Ellen Alleyne – to the Pre-Raphaelite journal, *The Germ*. Her most famous work, *Goblin Market*, appeared in 1862. In it, and in subsequent works, she demonstrated her idiosyncratic style, technical virtuosity and sense of the fantastic, as well as the religious concerns which, as a High Anglican, characterized her life and literary output. Frequent illness caused her to become somewhat reclusive, and many of her poems express a sense of introspection that has resulted in her being considered melancholy. Family deaths and personal disappointments may have contributed to this tendency: she was engaged to the Pre-Raphaelite painter James Collinson, and had other relationships, but never married. Her later collections include *The Prince's Progress* (1866) and *A Pageant* (1881), as well as nursery rhymes and works for children, among them *Sing-Song* (1872) and *Speaking Likenesses* (1874). Christina Rossetti died in London on 29 December 1894 and was buried in the family plot at Highgate Cemetery.

PART ONE

WHAT IS LOVE?

*F*or what is knowledge duly weighed?
  Knowledge is strong, but love is sweet;
Yea all the progress he had made
Was but to learn that all is small
Save love, for love is all in all.

FROM The Convent Threshold

JUDGE NOTHING BEFORE THE TIME

*L*ove understands the mystery, whereof
　　We can but spell a surface history:
Love knows, remembers: let us trust in Love:
　　Love understands the mystery.

　　Love weighs the event, the long pre-history,
Measures the depth beneath, the height above,
　　The mystery, with the ante-mystery.

To love and to be grieved befits a dove
　　Silently telling her bead-history:
Trust all to Love, be patient and approve:
　　Love understands the mystery.

QUINQUAGESIMA

*L*ove is alone the worthy law of love:
  All other laws have presupposed a taint:
  Love is the law from kindled saint to saint,
From lamb to lamb, from dove to answering dove.
Love is the motive of all things that move.
  Harmonious by free will without constraint:
  Love learns and teaches: love shall man acquaint
With all he lacks, which all his lack is love.
Because Love is the fountain, I discern
  The stream as love: for what but love should flow
  From fountain Love? not bitter from the sweet!
  I ignorant, have I laid claim to know?
  Oh teach me, Love, such knowledge as is meet
For one to know who is fain to love and learn.

ETERNAL LOVE

*P*iteous my rhyme is
    What while I muse of love and pain,
Of love mis-spent, of love in vain,
Of love that is not loved again:
   And is this all then?
   As long as time is,
Love loveth. Time is but a span,
The dalliance space of dying man:
And is this all immortals can?
   The gain were small then.

   Love loves for ever,
And finds a sort of joy in pain,
And gives with nought to take again,
And loves too well to end in vain:
   Is the gain small then?
   Love laughs at 'never,'
Outlives our life, exceeds the span
Appointed to mere mortal man:
All which love is and does and can
   Is all in all then.

EVERY ONE THAT IS PERFECT
SHALL BE AS HIS MASTER

*H*ow can one man, how can all men,
　　How can we be like St. Paul,
Like St. John, or like St. Peter,
　　Like the least of all
　　Blessed Saints? for we are small.

Love can make us like St. Peter,
　　Love can make us like St. Paul,
Love can make us like the blessed
　　Bosom friend of all,
　　Great St. John, tho' we are small

Love which clings and trusts and worships,
　　Love which rises from a fall,
Love which, prompting glad obedience,
　　Labours most of all,
　　Love makes great the great and small.

LOVE LIES BLEEDING

*L*ove, that is dead and buried, yesterday
    Out of his grave rose up before my face;
  No recognition in his look, no trace
Of memory in his eyes dust-dimmed and grey;
While I, remembering, found no word to say,
  But felt my quickened heart leap in its place;
  Caught afterglow thrown back from long-set days,
Caught echoes of all music past away.
Was this indeed to meet? – I mind me yet
  In youth we met when hope and love were quick,
    We parted with hope dead but love alive:
  I mind me how we parted then heart-sick,
    Remembering, loving, hopeless, weak to strive: –
Was this to meet? Not so, we have not met.

Love is all happiness, love is all beauty,
  Love is the crown of flaxen heads and hoary;
Love is the only everlasting duty;
And love is chronicled in endless story,
  And kindles endless glory.

LOVE ATTACKED

*L*ove is more sweet than flowers,
　　But sooner dying;
Warmer than sunny hours,
　　But faster flying;

Softer than music whispers,
　　Springing with day,
To murmur till the vespers,
　　Then die away;

More kind than friendship's greeting,
　　But as untrue;
Brighter than hope, but fleeting
　　More swiftly too.

Like breath of summer breezes
　　Gently it sighs,
But soon alas one ceases,
　　The other dies:

And like an inundation
　　It leaves behind
An utter desolation
　　Of heart and mind.

Who then would court Love's presence,
　　If here below
It can but be the essence
　　Of restless woe?

Returned or unrequited,
　　'Tis still the same;
The flame was never lighted,
　　Or sinks the flame.

Yet all, both fools and sages,
  Have felt its power,
In distant lands and ages, –
  Here, at this hour.

Then what from fear and weeping
  Shall give me rest?
Oh tell me, ye who sleeping
  At length are blest!

In answer to my crying,
  Sounds like incense
Rose from the earth, replying,
  'Indifference.'

LOVE AND HOPE

*L*ove for ever dwells in heaven, –
   Hope entereth not there.
  To despairing man Love's given, –
   Hope dwells not with despair.
Love reigneth high, and reigneth low, and
   reigneth everywhere.

  In the inmost heart Love dwelleth, –
   It may not quenchèd be;
  E'en when the life-blood welleth,
   Its fond effects we see
In the name that leaves the lips the last – fades last
   from memory.

  And when we shall awaken,
   Ascending to the sky,
  Though Hope shall have forsaken,
   Sweet Love shall never die:
For perfect Love and perfect bliss shall be our lot
   on high.

LOVE DEFENDED

*W*ho extols a wilderness?
    Who hath praised indifference?
Foolish one, thy words are sweet,
    But devoid of sense.

As the man who ne'er hath seen,
Or as he who cannot hear,
Is the heart that hath no part
    In Love's hope and fear.

True, the blind do not perceive
The unsightly things around;
True, the deaf man trembleth not
    At an awful sound.

But the face of heaven and earth,
And the murmur of the main,
Surely are a recompense
    For a little pain.

So, though Love may not be free
Always from a taint of grief,
If its sting is very sharp,
    Great is its relief.

AT LAST

*M*any have sung of love a root of bane:
   While to my mind a root of balm it is,
  For love at length breeds love; sufficient bliss
For life and death and rising up again.
Surely when light of Heaven makes all things plain,
  Love will grow plain with all its mysteries;
  Nor shall we need to fetch from over seas
Wisdom or wealth or pleasure safe from pain.
  Love in our borders, love within our heart,
  Love all in all, we then shall bide at rest,
  Ended for ever life's unending quest,
  Ended for ever effort, change, and fear:
Love all in all; – no more that better part
  Purchased, but at the cost of all things here.

GROWN AND FLOWN

I loved my love from green of Spring
    Until sere Autumn's fall;
But now that leaves are withering
    How should one love at all?
    One heart's too small
For hunger, cold, love, everything.

I loved my love on sunny days
    Until late Summer's wane;
But now that frost begins to glaze
    How should one love again?
    Nay, love and pain
Walk wide apart in diverse ways.

I loved my love – alas to see
    That this should be, alas!
I thought that this could scarcely be,
    Yet has it come to pass:
    Sweet sweet love was,
Now bitter bitter grown to me.

THESE ARE LOVE

Our heaven must be within ourselves,
   Our home and heaven the work of faith
All thro' this race of life which shelves
          Downward to death.

So faith shall build the boundary wall,
   And hope shall plant the secret bower,
That both may show magnifical
          With gem and flower.

While over all a dome must spread,
   And love shall be that dome above;
And deep foundations must be laid,
          And these are love.

PART TWO

I HAD A
LOVE...

My heart is like a singing bird
    Whose nest is in a water'd shoot;
My heart is like an apple tree
    Whose boughs are bent with thickset fruit;
My heart is like a rainbow shell
    That paddles in a halcyon sea;
My heart is gladder than all these
    Because my love is come to me.

FROM *A BIRTHDAY*

A PAUSE

They made the chamber sweet with flowers
   and leaves,
    And the bed sweet with flowers on which I lay;
    While my soul, love-bound, loitered on its way.
I did not hear the birds about the eaves,
Nor hear the reapers talk among the sheaves:
    Only my soul kept watch from day to day,
    My thirsty soul kept watch for one away: –
Perhaps he loves, I thought, remembers, grieves.
At length there came the step upon the stair,
    Upon the lock the old familiar hand:
Then first my spirit seemed to scent the air
    Of Paradise; then first the tardy sand
Of time ran golden; and I felt my hair
    Put on a glory, and my soul expand.

FROM
GOBLIN MARKET

*G*olden head by golden head,
   Like two pigeons in one nest
   Folded in each other's wings,
They lay down in their curtained bed:
Like two blossoms on one stem,
Like two flakes of new-fall'n snow,
Like two wands of ivory
Tipped with gold for awful kings.
Moon and stars gazed in at them,
Wind sang to them lullaby,
Lumbering owls forebore to fly,
Not a bat flapped to and fro
Round their nest:
Cheek to cheek and breast to breast
Locked together in one nest.

SONG

*I*t is not for her even brow
   And shining yellow hair,
But it is for her tender eyes
   I think my love so fair:
Her tell-tale eyes that smile and weep
As frankly as they wake and sleep.

It is not for her rounded cheek
   I love and fain would win,
But it is for the blush that comes
   Straight from the heart within:
The honest blush of maiden shame
That blushes without thought of blame.

So in my dreams I never hear
   Her song, although she sings
As if a choir of spirits swept
   From earth with throbbing wings:
I only hear the simple voice
Whose love makes many hearts rejoice.

FORGET ME NOT

'Forget me not, forget me not!'
  The maiden once did say,
When to some far-off battlefield
  Her lover sped away.

'Forget me not, forget me not!'
  Says now the chamber-maid,
When the traveller on his journey
  No more will be delayed.

ANNIE

*A*nnie is fairer than her kith
  And kinder than her kin:
He eyes are like the open heaven
  Holy and pure from sin:
Her heart is like an ordered house
  Good fairies harbour in:
Oh happy he who wins the love
  That I can never win!

Her sisters stand as hyacinths
   Around the perfect rose:
They bloom and open to the full,
   My bud will scarce unclose.
They are for every butterfly
   That comes and sips and goes:
My bud hides in the tender green
   Most sweet and hardly shows.

Oh cruel kindness in soft eyes
   That are no more than kind,
On which I gave my heart away
   Till the tears make me blind!
How is it others find the way
   That I can never find
To make her laugh that sweetest laugh
   Which leaves all else behind?

Her hair is like the golden corn
   A low wind breathes upon:
Or like the golden harvest-moon
   When all the mists are gone:
Or like a stream with golden sands
   On which the sun has shone
Day after day in summertime
   Ere autumn leaves are wan.

I will not tell her that I love,
   Lest she should turn away
With sorrow in her tender heart
   Which now is light and gay.
I will not tell her that I love,
   Lest she should turn and say
That we must meet no more again
   For many a weary day.

ELEANOR

*C*herry-red her mouth was,
    Morning-blue her eye,
Lady-slim her little waist
    Rounded prettily;
    And her sweet smile of gladness
    Made every heart rejoice:
But sweeter even than her smile
    The tones were of her voice.

Sometimes she spoke, sometimes she sang;
    And evermore the sound
Floated, a dreamy melody,
    Upon the air around;
    As though a wind were singing
    Far up beside the sun,
    Till sound and warmth and glory
    Were blended all in one.

    Her hair was long and golden,
    And clustered unconfined
Over a forehead high and white
    That spoke a noble mind.
Her little hand, her little foot,
    Were ready evermore
To hurry forth to meet a friend;
    She smiling at the door.

But if she sang or if she spoke,
    'Twas music soft and grand,
As though a distant singing sea
    Broke on a tuneful strand;
    As though a blessed Angel
    Were singing a glad song,
Halfway between the earth and heaven
    Joyfully borne along.

IS AND WAS

She was whiter than the ermine
  That half shadowed neck and hand,
And her tresses were more golden
   Than their golden band;
Snowy ostrich plumes she wore;
Yet I almost loved her more
In the simple time before.

Then she plucked the stately lilies,
Knowing not she was more fair,
And she listened to the skylark
   In the morning air.
Then, a kerchief all her crown,
She looked for the acorns brown,
Bent their bough, and shook them down.

Then she thought of Christmas holly
And of Maybloom in sweet May;
Then she loved to pick the cherries
   And to turn the hay.
She was humble then and meek,
And the blush upon her cheek
Told of much she could not speak.

Now she is a noble lady
With calm voice not over loud;
Very courteous in her action,
   Yet you think her proud;
Much too haughty to affect;
Too indifferent to direct
Or be angry or suspect;
Doing all from self-respect.

MARIANA

Not for me marring or making,
  Not for me giving or taking;
    I love my Love and he loves not me,
I love my Love and my heart is breaking.

Sweet is Spring in its lovely showing,
Sweet the violet veiled in blowing,
  Sweet it is to love and be loved;
Ah sweet knowledge beyond my knowing!

Who sighs for love sighs but for pleasure,
Who wastes for love hoards up a treasure;
  Sweet to be loved and take no count,
Sweet it is to love without measure.

Sweet my Love whom I loved to try for,
Sweet my Love whom I love and sigh for,
  Will you once love me and sigh for me,
You my Love whom I love and die for?

'DOETH WELL... DOETH BETTER'

My love whose heart is tender said to me,
  'A moon lacks light except her sun befriend her.
'Let us keep tryst in heaven, dear Friend,' said she,
  My love whose heart is tender.

  From such a loftiness no words could bend her:
Yet still she spoke of 'us' and spoke as 'we,'
  Her hope substantial, while my hope grew slender.

Now keeps she tryst beyond earth's utmost sea,
  Wholly at rest, tho' storms should toss and rend her;
And still she keeps my heart and keeps its key,
  My love whose heart is tender.

A BRIDE SONG

T hrough the vales to my love!
To the happy small nest of home
Green from basement to roof;
Where the honey-bees come
To the window-sill flowers
   And dive from above
Safe from the spider that weaves
   Her warp and her woof
   In some outermost leaves.

Through the vales to my love!
  In sweet April hours
  All rainbows and showers,
  While dove answers dove, –
  In beautiful May,
  When the orchards are tender
  And frothing with flowers, –
  In opulent June
  When the wheat stands up slender
  By sweet-smelling hay,
  And half the sun's splendour
  Descends to the moon.

Through the vales to my love!
Where the turf is so soft to the feet
  And the thyme makes it sweet,
  And the stately foxglove
Hangs silent its exquisite bells;
  And where water wells
  The greenness grows greener,
  And bulrushes stand
  Round a lily to screen her.

Nevertheless, if this land,
Like a garden to smell and to sight,
Were turned to a desert of sand;
  Stripped bare of delight,
  All its best gone to worst,
  For my feet no repose,
No water to comfort my thirst,
And heaven like a furnace above, –
  The desert would be
As gushing of waters to me,
The wilderness be as a rose,
  If it led me to thee,
    O my love.

LOVE FROM THE NORTH

I had a love in soft south land,
   Beloved through April far in May;
He waited on my lightest breath,
   And never dared to say me nay.

He saddened if my cheer was sad,
   But gay he grew if I was gay;
We never differed on a hair,
   My yes his yes, my nay his nay.

The wedding hour was come, the aisles
   Were flushed with sun and flowers that day;
I pacing balanced in my thoughts:
   'It's quite too late to think of nay.' –

My bridegroom answered in his turn,
   Myself had almost answered 'yea:'
When through the flashing nave I heard
   A struggle and resounding 'nay.'

Bridemaids and bridegroom shrank in fear,
   But I stood high who stood at bay:
'And if I answer yea, fair Sir,
   What man art thou to bar with nay?'

He was a strong man from the north,
   Light-locked, with eyes of dangerous grey:
'Put yea by for another time
   In which I will not say thee nay.'

He took me in his strong white arms,
   He bore me on his horse away
O'er crag, morass, and hairbreadth pass,
   But never asked me yea or nay.

He made me fast with book and bell,
  With links of love he makes me stay;
Till now I've neither heart nor power
  Nor will not wish to say him nay.

THE DREAM

*R*est, rest; the troubled breast
   Panteth evermore for rest: –
     Be it sleep or be it death,
  Rest is all it coveteth.

Tell me, dost thou remember the old time
   We sat together by that sunny stream,
And dreamed our happiness was too sublime
    Only to be a dream?

Gazing, till steadfast gazing made us blind,
   We watched the fishes leaping at their play;
Thinking our love too tender and too kind
    Ever to pass away.

And some of all our thoughts were true at least
   What time we thought together by that stream;
Thy happiness has evermore increased, –
    My love was not a dream.

And, now that thou art gone, I often sit
   On its green margin, for thou once wert there;
And see the clouds that, floating over it,
    Darken the quiet air.

Yes oftentimes I sit beside it now,
   Hearkening the wavelets ripple o'er the sands;
Until again I hear thy whispered vow
    And feel thy pressing hands.

Then the bright sun seems to stand still in heaven,
   The stream sings gladly as it onwards flows,
The rushes grow more green, the grass more even,
    Blossoms the budding rose.

I say: 'It is a joy-dream; I will take it;
    He is not gone – he will return to me.'
What found'st thou in my heart that thou shouldst
        break it? –
        How have I injured thee?

Oh I am weary of life's passing show,
    Its pageant and its pain,
I would I could lie down lone in my woe,
    Ne'er to rise up again;
I would I could lie down where none might know;
    For truly love is vain.

Truly love's vain; but oh how vainer still
    Is that which is not love, but seems!
Concealed indifference, a covered ill,
    A very dream of dreams.

PART THREE

MOTHER AND CHILD

*A*ngels at the foot,
  And Angels at the head,
And like a curly little lamb
  My pretty babe in bed.

———————

Love me, — I love you,
  Love me, my baby;
Sing it high, sing it low,
  Sing it as may be.

———————

Mother's arms under you,
  Her eyes above you;
Sing it high, sing it low,
  Love me, — I love you.

Rhymes dedicated without permission
to the baby who suggested them

HOLY INNOCENTS

Sleep, little Baby, sleep;
  The holy Angels love thee,
And guard thy bed, and keep
  A blessed watch above thee.
No spirit can come near
  Nor evil beast to harm thee:
Sleep, Sweet, devoid of fear
  Where nothing need alarm thee.

The Love which doth not sleep,
  The eternal Arms surround thee:
The Shepherd of the sheep
  In perfect love hath found thee.
Sleep through the holy night,
  Christ-kept from snare and sorrow,
Until thou wake to light
  And love and warmth to-morrow.

VALENTINES TO MY MOTHER

1876

*F*airer than younger beauties, more beloved
   Than many a wife,
By stress of Time's vicissitudes unmoved
   From settled calm of life;

Endearing rectitude to those who watch
   The verdict of your face,
Raising and making gracious those who catch
   A semblance of your grace:

With kindly lips of welcome, and with pleased
   Propitious eyes benign,
Accept a kiss of homage from your least
   Last Valentine.

1877

Own Mother dear,
We all rejoicing here
Wait for each other,
Daughter for Mother,
Sister for Brother,
Till each dear face appear
Transfigured by Love's flame
   Yet still the same, –
   The same yet new, –
   My face to you,
   Your face to me,
Made lovelier by Love's flame
   But still the same;
   Most dear to see
In halo of Love's flame,
   Because the same.

1878

Blessed Dear and Heart's Delight,
  Companion, Friend, and Mother mine
    Round whom my fears and love entwine, –
      With whom I hope to stand and sing
      Where angels form the outer ring
Round singing Saints who, clad in white,
Know no more of day or night
    Or death or any changeful thing,
    Or anything that is not love,
  Human love and Love Divine, –
    Bid me to that tryst above,
      Bless your Valentine.

1882

My blessed Mother dozing in her chair
  On Christmas Day seemd an embodied Love,
A comfortable Love with soft brown hair
  Softened and silvered to a tint of dove;
A better sort of Venus with an air
  Angelical from thoughts that dwell above;
A wiser Pallas in whose body fair
  Enshrined a blessed soul looks out thereof.
Winter brought holly then; now Spring has brought
  Paler and frailer snowdrops shivering;
And I have brought a simple humble thought –
I her devoted duteous Valentine –
  A lifelong thought which thrills this song I sing,
A lifelong love to this dear Saint of mine.

1883

A world of change and loss, a world of death,
Of heart and eyes that fail, of labouring breath,
Of pains to bear and painful deeds to do: —
Nevertheless a world of life to come
And love; where you're at home, while in our home
Your Valentine rejoices, having you.

1884

Another year of joy and grief,
   Another year of hope and fear:
O Mother, is life long or brief?
   We hasten while we linger here.

But, since we linger, love me still
   And bless me still, O Mother mine,
While hand in hand we scale life's hill,
   You guide, and I your Valentine.

1885

All the Robin Redbreasts
   Have lived the winter through,
Jenny Wrens have pecked their fill
   And found a work to do;
   Families of Sparrows
   Have weathered wind and storm
With Rabbit on the stony hill
   And Hare upon her form.

   You and I, my Mother,
   Have lived the winter through,
And still we play our daily parts
   And still find work to do:
   And still the cornfields flourish,
   The olive and the vine,
And still you reign my Queen of Hearts
   And I'm your Valentine

TO MY MOTHER

ON THE ANNIVERSARY OF HER BIRTH

(Presented with a Nosegay)

*T*o-day's your natal day;
   Sweet flowers I bring:
Mother, accept I pray
   My offering.

And may you happy live,
   And long us bless;
Receiving as you give
   Great happiness.

PART FOUR

THE LOVE OF NATURE

*I*n Springtime when the leaves are young,
Clear dewdrops gleam like jewels, hung
On boughs the fair birds roost among.

When Summer comes with sweet unrest,
Birds weary of their mother's breast,
And look abroad and leave the nest.

In Autumn ere the waters freeze,
The swallows fly across the seas: –
If we could fly away with these!

In Winter when the birds are gone,
The sun himself looks starved and wan,
And starved the snow he shines upon.

Seasons

THE FIRST SPRING DAY

I wonder if the sap is stirring yet,
  If wintry birds are dreaming of a mate,
If frozen snowdrops feel as yet the sun
And crocus fires are kindling one by one:
    Sing, robin, sing;
I still am sore in doubt concerning Spring.

I wonder if the Springtide of this year
Will bring another Spring both lost and dear;
If heart and spirit will find out their Spring,
Or if the world alone will bud and sing:
    Sing, hope, to me;
Sweet notes, my hope, soft notes for memory.

The sap will surely quicken soon or late,
The tardiest bird will twitter to a mate;

So Spring must dawn again with warmth and
    bloom,
Or in this world or in the world to come:
    Sing, voice of Spring,
Till I too blossom and rejoice and sing.

THE LAMBS OF GRASMERE

The upland flocks grew starved and thinned:
  Their shepherds scarce could feed the lambs
Whose milkless mothers butted them,
  Or who were orphaned of their dams.
The lambs athirst for mother's milk
  Filled all the place with piteous sounds:
Their mothers' bones made white for miles
  The pastureless wet pasture grounds.

Day after day, night after night,
  From lamb to lamb the shepherds went,
With teapots for the bleating mouths,
  Instead of nature's nourishment.
The little shivering gaping things
  Soon knew the step that brought them aid,
And fondled the protecting hand,
  And rubbed it with a woolly head.

Then, as the days waxed on to weeks,
  It was a pretty sight to see
These lambs with frisky heads and tails
  Skipping and leaping on the lea,
Bleating in tender trustful tones,
  Resting on rocky crag or mound,
And following the beloved feet
  That once had sought for them and found.

These very shepherds of their flocks,
  These loving lambs so meek to please,
Are worthy of recording words
  And honour in their due degrees:
So I might live in a hundred years,
  And roam from strand to foreign strand,
Yet not forget this flooded spring
  And scarce-saved lambs of Westmoreland.

ANOTHER SPRING

*I*f I might see another Spring,
   I'd not plant summer flowers and wait:
I'd have my crocuses at once,
My leafless pink mezereons,
   My chill-veined snowdrops, choicer yet
   My white or azure violet,
Leaf-nested primrose; anything
   To blow at once, not late.

If I might see another Spring,
   I'd listen to the daylight birds
That build their nests and pair and sing,
Nor wait for mateless nightingale;
   I'd listen to the lusty herds,
   The ewes with lambs as white as snow,
I'd find out music in the hail
   And all the winds that blow.

If I might see another Spring —
   Oh stinging comment on my past
That all my past results in 'if' —
   If I might see another Spring
I'd laugh to-day, to-day is brief;
I would not wait for anything:
   I'd use to-day that cannot last,
   Be glad to-day and sing.

CHILD'S TALK IN APRIL

I wish you were a pleasant wren,
   And I your small accepted mate;
How we'd look down on toilsome men!
   We'd rise and go to bed at eight
   Or it may be not quite so late.

Then you should see the nest I'd build,
   The wondrous nest for you and me;
The outside rough perhaps, but filled
   With wool and down, ah you should see
   The cosy nest that it would be.

We'd have our change of hope and fear,
   Small quarrels, reconcilements sweet:
I'd perch by you to chirp and cheer,
   Or hop about on active feet,
   And fetch you dainty bits to eat.

We'd be so happy by the day,
   So safe and happy through the night,
We both should feel, and I should say,
   It's all one season of delight,
And we'll make merry whilst we may.

Perhaps some day there'd be an egg
   When spring had blossomed from the snow:
I'd stand triumphant on one leg;
   Like chanticleer I'd almost crow
   To let our little neighbours know.

Next you should sit and I would sing
Through lengthening days of sunny spring;
   Till, if you wearied of the task,
I'd sit; and you should spread your wing
   From bough to bough; I'd sit and bask.

Fancy the breaking of the shell,
　　The chirp, the chickens wet and bare,
The untried proud paternal swell;
　　And you with housewife-matron air
　　Enacting choicer bills of fare.

Fancy the embryo coats of down,
　　The gradual feathers soft and sleek;
Till clothed and strong from tail to crown,
　　With virgin warblings in their beak,
　　They too go forth to soar and seek.

So would it last an April through
And early summer fresh with dew, –
　　Then should we part and live as twain;
Love-time would bring me back to you,
　　And build our happy nest again.

A WISH

I wish I were a little bird
　　That out of sight doth soar;
　I wish I were a song once heard
　　　But often pondered o'er,
　Or shadow of a lily stirred
　By wind upon the floor,
　Or echo of a loving word
　　Worth all that went before,
　Or memory of a hope deferred
　　That springs again no more.

VENUS'S LOOKING-GLASS

I marked where lovely Venus and her court
   With song and dance and merry laugh went by;
      Weightless, their wingless feet seemed made
         to fly,
Bound from the ground, and in mid air to sport.
Left far behind I heard the dolphins snort,
      Tracking their goddess with a wistful eye,
      Around whose head white doves rose, wheeling
         high
Or low, and cooed after their tender sort.
All this I saw in Spring. Through summer heat
   I saw the lovely Queen of Love no more.
      But when flushed Autumn through the woodlands
         went
I spied sweet Venus walk amid the wheat:
      Whom seeing, every harvester gave o'er
      His toil, and laught and hoped and was content.

DREAM-LOVE

*Y*oung Love lies sleeping
  In May-time of the year,
Among the lilies,
  Lapped in the tender light:
White lambs come grazing,
  White doves come building there;
And round about him
  The May-bushes are white.

Soft moss the pillow
  For oh a softer cheek;
Board leaves cast shadow
  Upon the heavy eyes:
There winds and waters
  Grow lulled and scarcely speak;
There twilight lingers
  The longest in the skies.

Young Love lies dreaming;
  But who shall tell the dream?
A perfect sunlight
  On rustling forest tips;
Or perfect moonlight
  Upon a rippling stream;
Or perfect silence,
  Or song of cherished lips.

Burn odours round him
  To fill the drowsy air;
Weave silent dances
  Around him to and fro;
For oh in waking
  The sights are not so fair,
And song and silence
  Are not like these below.

Young Love lies dreaming
　Till summer days are gone, –
Dreaming and drowsing
　Away to perfect sleep:
He sees the beauty
　Sun hath not looked upon,
And tastes the fountain
　Unutterably deep.

Him perfect music
　Doth hush unto his rest,
And through the pauses
　The perfect silence calms:
Oh poor the voices
　Of earth from east to west,
And poor earth's stillness
　Between her stately palms!

Young Love lies drowsing
　Away to poppied death;
Cool shadows deepen
　Across the sleeping face:
So fails the summer
　With warm delicious breath;
And what hath autumn
　To give us in its place?

Draw close the curtains
　Of branchèd evergreen;
Change cannot touch them
　With fading fingers sere:
Here the first violets
　Perhaps will bud unseen,
And a dove, may be,
　Return to nestle here.

SUMMER

*W*inter is cold-hearted,
　　Spring is yea and nay,
Autumn is a weathercock
　　Blown every way.
　　Summer days for me
When every leaf is on its tree;

　　When Robin's not a beggar
　　And Jenny Wren's a bride,
And larks hang singing, singing, singing,
　　Over the wheat-fields wide,
　　And anchored lilies ride,
　　And the pendulum spider
　　Swings from side to side;

And blue-black beetles transact business,
　　And gnats fly in a host,
And furry caterpillars hasten
　　That no time be lost,
　　And moths grow fat and thrive,
　　And ladybirds arrive.

　　Before green apples blush,
　　Before green nuts embrown,
　　Why one day in the country
　　Is worth a month in town;
　　Is worth a day and a year
Of the dusty, musty, lag-last fashion
　　That days drone elsewhere.

IN THE LANE

*W*hen my love came home to me,
　　Pleasant summer bringing,
Every tree was out in leaf,
　　Every bird was singing.

There I met her in the lane
　　By those waters gleamy,
Met her toward the fall of day,
　　Warm and dear and dreamy.
Did I loiter in the lane?
　　None was there to see me.

Only roses in the hedge,
　　Lilies on the river,
Saw our greeting fast and fond,
　　Counted gift and giver,
Saw me take her to my home,
　　Take her home for ever.

LINES TO MY GRANDFATHER

*D*ear Grandpapa, – To be obedient,
   I'll try and write a letter;
Which (as I hope you'll deem expedient)
   Must serve for lack of better.

My Muse of late was not prolific;
   And sometimes I must feel
To make a verse a task terrific
   Rather of woe than weal.

As I have met with no adventure
   Of wonder and refulgence,
I must write plain things at a venture,
   And trust to your indulgence.

The apple-tree is showing
   Its blossom of bright red,
With a soft colour glowing
   Upon its leafy bed.

The pear-tree's pure white blossom
   Like stainless snow is seen;
And all earth's genial bosom
   Is clothed with varied green.

The fragrant may is blooming,
   The yellow cowslip blows;
Among its leaves entombing
   Peeps forth the pale primrose.

The king-cup flowers and daisies
   Are opening hard by;
And many another raises
   Its head, to please and die.

I love the gay wild flowers
   Waving in fresh Spring air:—
Give me uncultured bowers
   Before the bright parterre.

And now my letter is concluded;
   To do well I have striven;
And, though news is well-nigh excluded,
   I hope to be forgiven.

With love to all the beautiful
   And those who cannot slaughter,
I sign myself — Your dutiful
   Affectionate grand-daughter.

GONE FOR EVER

O happy rosebud blooming
   Upon they parent tree,
Nay, thou art too presuming;
For soon the earth entombing
   Thy faded charms shall be,
And the chill damp consuming.

O happy skylark springing
   Up to the broad blue sky,
Too fearless in thy winging,
Too gladsome in thy singing,
   Thou also soon shalt lie
Where no sweet notes are ringing.

And through life's shine and shower
   We shall have joy and pain:
But in the summer bower
And at the morning hour
   We still shall look in vain
For the same bird and flower.

AUTUMN

*C*are flieth,
  Hope and Fear together:
  Love dieth
In the Autumn weather.

  For a friend
  Even Care is pleasant:
  When Fear doth end
  Hope is no more present:
Autumn silences the turtle-dove: –
In blank Autumn who could speak of love?

AUTUMN

I dwell alone – I dwell alone, alone,
    Whilst fully my river flows down to the sea,
   Gilded with flashing boats
    That bring no friend to me:
O love-songs, gurgling from a hundred throats,
   O love-pangs, let me be.

Fair fall the freighted boats which gold and stone
   And spices bear to sea:
Slim gleaming maidens swell their mellow notes,
   Love-promising, entreating –
   Ah sweet but fleeting –

   Beneath the shivering, snow-white sails.
   Hush! the wind flags and fails –
Hush! they will lie becalmed in sight of strand –
   Sight of my strand, where I do dwell alone;
Their songs wake singing echoes in my land –
   They cannot hear me moan.

   One latest, solitary swallow flies
    Across the sea, rough autumn-tempest-tost:
    Poor bird, shall it be lost?
   Dropped down into this uncongenial sea,
    With no kind eyes
    To watch it while it dies,
   Unguessed, uncared for, free:
    Set free at last,
    The short pang past,
In sleep, in death, in dreamless sleep locked fast.

Mine avenue is all a growth of oaks,
   Some rent by thunder strokes,
Some rustling leaves and acorns in the breeze;
   Fair fall my fertile trees,
That rear their goodly heads, and live at ease.

A spider's web blocks all mine avenue;
  He catches down and foolish painted flies,
    That spider wary and wise.
Each morn it hangs a rainbow strung with dew
  Betwixt boughs green with sap,
  So fair, few creatures guess it is a trap:
  I will not mar the web,
Though sad I am to see the small lives ebb.

It shakes – my trees shake – for a wind is roused
  In cavern where it housed:
  Each white and quivering sail
  Of boats among the water-leaves
Hollows and strains in the full-throated gale:
  Each maiden sings again –
Each languid maiden, whom the calm
Had lulled to sleep with rest and spice and balm.
  Miles down my river to the sea
    They float and wane,
  Long miles away from me.

  Perhaps they say: 'She grieves,
Uplifted like a beacon on her tower.'
    Perhaps they say: 'One hour
More, and we dance among the golden sheaves.'
  Perhaps they say: 'One hour
    More, and we stand,
    Face to face, hand in hand;
Make haste, O slack gale, to the looked-for land!'

  My trees are not in flower,
  I have no bower,
  And gusty creaks my tower,
And lonesome, very lonesome, is my strand.

THREE SEASONS

'A cup for hope!' she said,
  In springtime ere the bloom was old;
The crimson wine was poor and cold
    By her mouth's richer red.

'A cup for love!' how low,
How soft the words; and all the while
Her blush was rippling with a smile
    Like summer after snow.

'A cup for memory!'
Cold cup that one must drain alone:
While autumn winds are up and moan
    Across the barren sea.

Hope, memory, love:
Hope for fair morn, and love for day,
And memory for the evening grey
    And solitary dove.

WINTER: MY SECRET

I tell my secret? No indeed, not I:
Perhaps some day, who knows?
But not to-day; it froze, and blows, and snows,
And you're too curious: fie!
You want to hear it? well:
Only, my secret's mine, and I won't tell.

Or, after all, perhaps there's none:
Suppose ther is no secret after all,
But only just my fun.
To-day's a nipping day, a biting day;
In which one wants a shawl,
A veil, a cloak, and other wraps:
I cannot ope to every one who taps,
And let the draughts come whistling through my
        hall;
Come bounding and surrounding me,
Come buffeting, astounding me,
Nipping and clipping through my wraps and all.
I wear my mask for warmth: who ever shows
His nose to Russian snows
To be pecked at by every wind that blows?
You would not peck? I thank you for good will,
Believe, but leave that truth untested still.

Spring's an expansive time: yet I don't trust
March with its peck of dust,
Nor April with its rainbow-crowned brief showers,
Nor even May, whose flowers
One frost may wither through the sunless hours.

Perhaps some languid summer day,
When drowsy birds sing less and less,
And golden fruit is ripening to excess,
If there's not too much sun nor too much cloud,
And the warm wind is neither still nor loud,
Perhaps my secret I may say,
Or you may guess.

WINTER

Sweet blackbird is silenced with chaffinch and thrush,
Only waistcoated robin still chirps in the bush:
Soft sun-loving swallows have mustered in force,
And winged to the spice-teeming southlands their course.

Plump housekeeper dormouse has tucked himself neat,
Just a brown ball in moss with a morsel to eat:
Armed hedgehog has huddled him into the hedge,
While frogs scarce miss freezing deep down in the sedge.

Soft swallows have left us alone in the lurch,
But robin sits whistling to us from his perch:
If I were red robin, I'd pipe you a tune
Would make you despise all the beauties of June.

But, since that cannot be, let us draw round the fire,
Munch chesnuts, tell stories, and stir the blaze higher:
We'll comfort pinched robin with crumbs, little man,
Till he sings us the very best song that he can.

PART FIVE

THE FAIREST FLOWERS

*L*ove is sweet, and so are flowers
  Blooming in bright summer bowers;
So are waters, clear and pure,
In some hidden fountain's store;
So is the soft southern breeze
Sighing low among the trees;
So is the bright queen of heaven
Reigning in the quiet even.
Yet the pallid moon may breed
Madness in man's feeble seed;
And the wind's soft influence
Often breathes the pestilence;
And the waves may sullied be
As they hurry to the sea;
Flowers soon must fade away:
Love endures but for a day.

LOVE EPHEMERAL

CONSIDER THE LILIES OF
THE FIELD

Flowers preach to us if we will hear:—
   The rose saith in the dewy morn:
'I am most fair;
Yet all my loveliness is born
Upon a thorn.'
The poppy saith amid the corn:
'Let but my scarlet head appear
And I am held in scorn;
Yet juice of subtle virtue lies
Within my cup of curious dyes.'
The lilies say: 'Behold how we
Preach without words of purity.'
The violets whisper from the shade
Which their own leaves have made:
'Men scent our fragrance on the air,
Yet take no heed
Of humble lessons we would read.'

But not alone the fairest flowers:
The merest grass
Along the roadside where we pass,
Lichen and moss and sturdy weed,
Tell of His love who sends the dew,
The rain and sunshine too,
To nourish one small seed.

CONFLUENTS

*A*s rivers seek the sea,
   Much more deep than they,
So my soul seeks thee
   Far away;
As running rivers moan
On their course alone,
   So I moan
   Left alone.

As the delicate rose
   To the sun's sweet strength
Doth herself unclose,
   Breadth and length;
So spreads my heart to thee
Unveiled utterly,
   I to thee
   Utterly.

As morning dew exhales
   Sunwards pure and free
So my spirit fails
   After thee.
As dew leaves not a trace
On the green earth's face;
   I, no trace
   On thy face.

Its goal the river knows,
   Dewdrops find a way,
Sunlight cheers the rose
   In her day:
Shall I, lone sorrow past,
Find thee at the last?
   Sorrow past,
   Thee at last?

A BED OF FORGET-ME-NOTS

*I*s Love so prone to change and rot
We are fain to rear Forget-me-not
By measure in a garden-plot? –

I love its growth at large and free
By untrod path and unlopped tree,
Or nodding by the unpruned hedge,
Or on the water's dangerous edge
Where flags and meadowsweet blow rank
With rushes on the quaking bank.

Love is not taught in learning's school,
Love is not parcelled out by rule:
Hath curb or call an answer got? –
So free must be Forget-me-not.
Give me the flame no dampness dulls,
The passion of the instinctive pulse,
Love steadfast as a fixèd star,
Tender as doves with nestlings are,
More large than time, more strong than death:
    This all creation travails of –
She groans not for a passing breath –
    This is Forget-me-not and Love.

THE ROSE

O rose, thou flower of flowers, thou fragrant
   wonder,
  Who shall describe thee in thy ruddy prime,
  Thy perfect fullness in the summertime,
When the pale leaves blushingly part asunder
And show the warm red heart lies glowing under?
  Thou shouldst bloom surely in some sunny clime,
  Untouched by blights and chilly winter's rime,
Where lightnings never flash nor peals the thunder.
And yet in happier spheres they cannot need thee
  So much as we do with our weight of woe;
Perhaps they would not tend, perhaps not heed thee,
  And thou wouldst lonely and neglected grow:
And He who is all wise, He hath decreed thee
  To gladden earth and cheer all hearts below.

THE SOLITARY ROSE

O happy rose, red rose, that bloomest lonely
 Where there are none to gather while they love thee;
That art perfumed by thine own fragrance only,
 Resting like incense round thee and above thee; —
Thou hearest nought save some pure stream that flows,
  O happy rose.

What though for thee no nightingales are singing?
 They chant one eve, but hush them in the
  morning.
Near thee no little moths and bees are winging
 To steal thy honey when the day is dawning; —
Thou keep'st thy sweetness till the twilight's close,
  O happy rose.

Then rest in peace, thou lone and lovely flower;
 Yea be thou glad, knowing that none are near thee,
To mar thy beauty in a wanton hour,
 And scatter all thy leaves nor deign to wear thee.
Securely in thy solitude repose,
  O happy rose.

QUEEN ROSE

*T*he jessamine shows like a star;
　　The lilies sway like sceptres slim;
Fair clematis from near and far
　　Sets forth its wayward tangled whim:
　　Curved meadowsweet blooms rich and dim; –
But yet a rose is fairer far.

The jessamine is odorous; so
　　Maid-lilies are, and clematis;
And where tall meadowsweet-flowers grow
　　A rare and subtle perfume is; –
　　What can there be more choice than these? –
A rose when it doth bud and blow.

Let others choose sweet jessamine,
　　Or weave their lily-crown aright,
And let who love it pluck and twine
　　Loose clematis, or draw delight
　　From meadowsweets' cluster downy white –
The rose, the perfect rose, be mine.